The Joy of
33 Recital Pieces
by Denes Agay

Includes a Compact Disc of all the pieces performed by Elaine Leber and Cecelia Wyatt.

Yorktown Music Press, Inc.
New York/London/Paris/Sydney/Copenhagen/Madrid/Tokyo/Berlin

Order No. YK 21934
US International Standard Book Number: 0.8256.8110.3
UK International Standard Book Number: 0.7119.9686.5

Exclusive Distributors:
Music Sales Corporation
257 Park Avenue South, New York, NY 10010 USA
Music Sales Limited
8/9 Frith Street, London W1D 3JB England
Music Sales Pty. Limited
120 Rothschild Street, Rosebery, Sydney, NSW 2018, Australia

Printed in the United States of America by
Vicks Lithograph and Printing Corporation

Contents

Here Comes the Circus!

Music by Denes Agay

Very bright

5

Barcolette

Music by Denes Agay

Moderately, with gentle motion

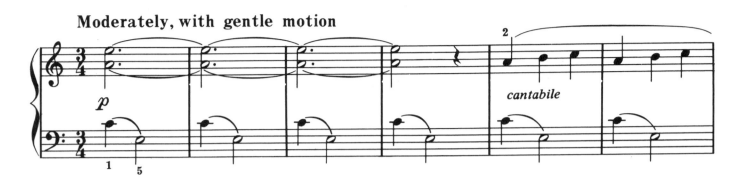

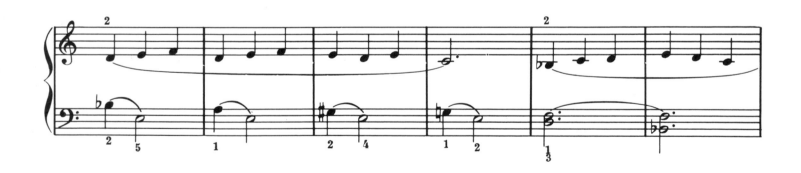

Puppet Polka

By Denes Agay

Very bright; with humor

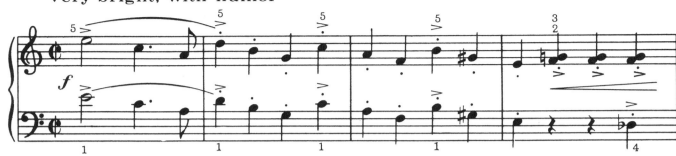

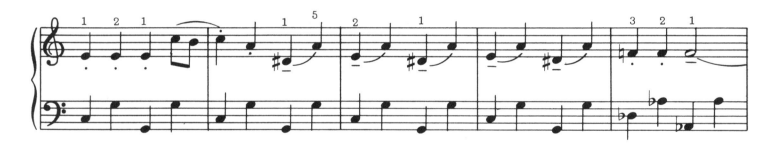

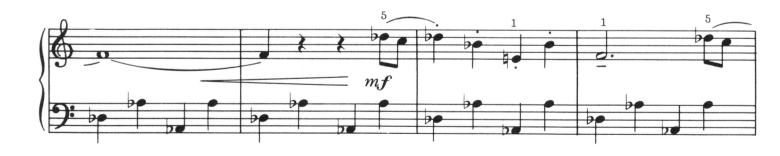

The Shepherds' Night Song

Music by Denes Agay

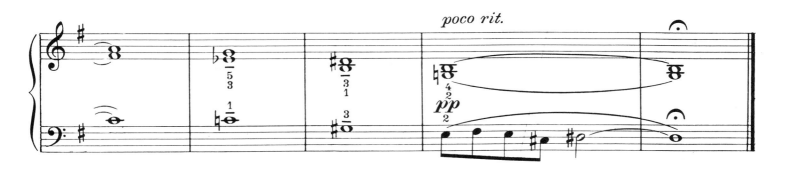

Lonely Waltz

By Denes Agay

Frolic

Music by Denes Agay

15

Evening and Morning
(Two Little Pastorales)
Music by Denes Agay

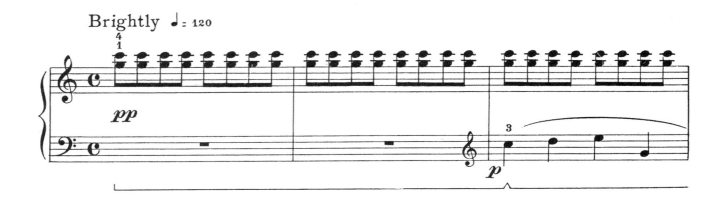

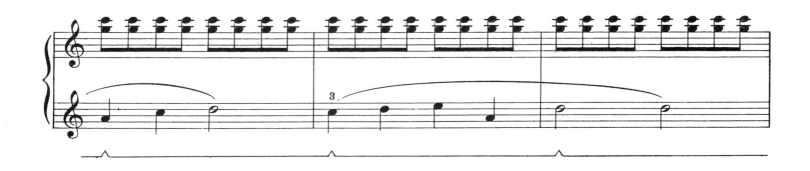

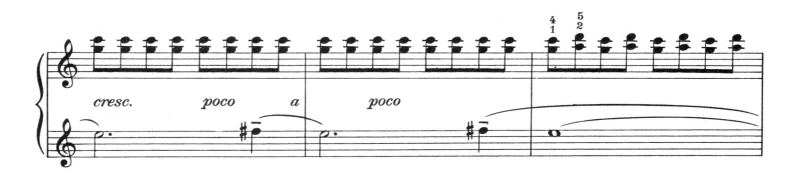

Music Box Rag

Music by Denes Agay

A Golden Valentine

Music by Denes Agay

Once Upon a Time

Music by Denes Agay

Andantino delicato

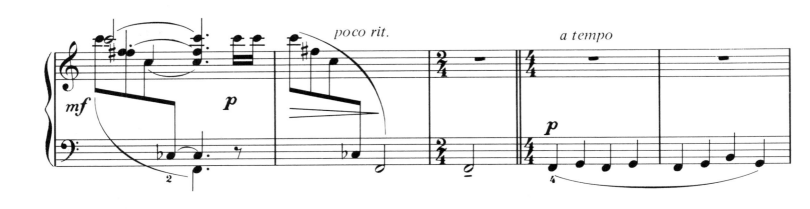

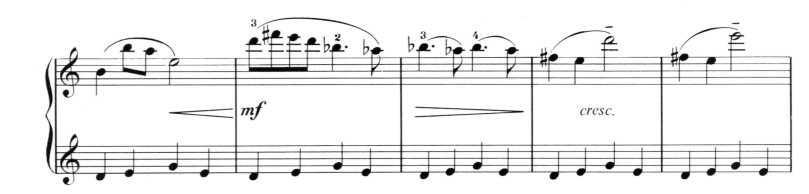

Variations on a Greeting Song

Music by Denes Agay

Allegretto cantabile (... Mozart)

Andante maestoso (...Beethoven)

Allegro

Allegretto (... Schubert)

stacc. sempre

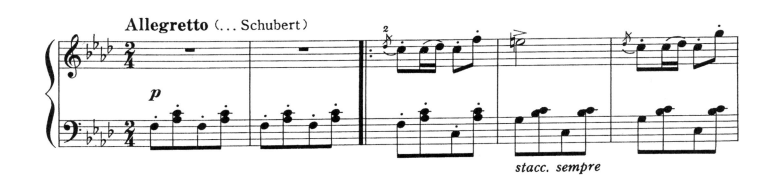

32

Andante con moto (…Chopin)

Moderately lively waltz (... Johann Strauss)

Lively March (... John Philip Sousa)

Con moto, delicato (... Debussy)

Slow, steady beat (... Ballad à la Gershwin)

38

Sonatina in a Classic Style

Music by Denes Agay

Lento, con molto espressione ♩ = ca 60

Optional repeat from 𝄋

44

Prelude on "The Star-Spangled Banner"

Music by Denes Agay

Flirtation Walk

Music by Denes Agay

Happily strutting

Più mosso

Little Rhapsody on "America the Beautiful"

Music by Denes Agay

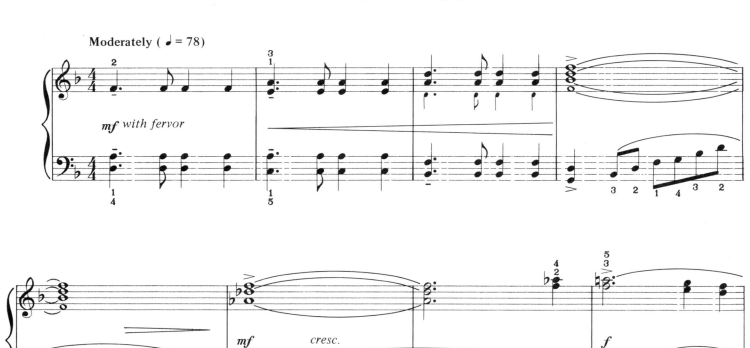

Blue Waltz

Music by Denes Agay

Moderately, with a lilt

Walkin' in the Rain

Music by Denes Agay

Comfortable walking tempo

Big-City Pastorale

Music by Denes Agay

The Memory of a Waltz

Music by Denes Agay

Andantino, molto rubato

Another Shade of Blue

Music by Denes Agay

Slowly, with a free lilt

Four Folk Tune Sonatinas

(Hungarian-American-Irish-Spanish)

Music by Denes Agay

Allegretto giocoso (♩ = 72)

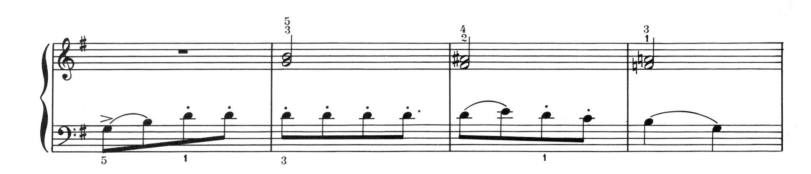

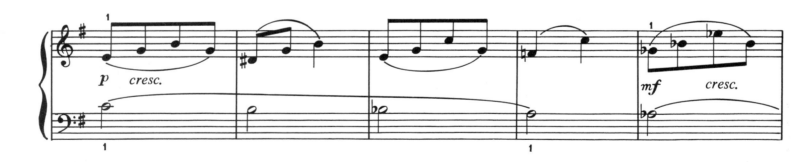

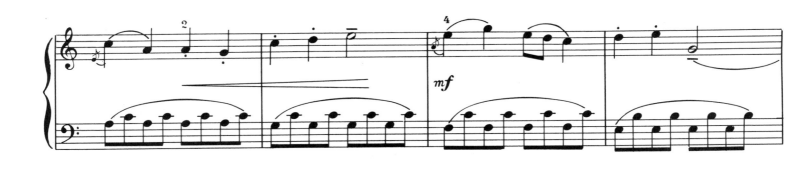

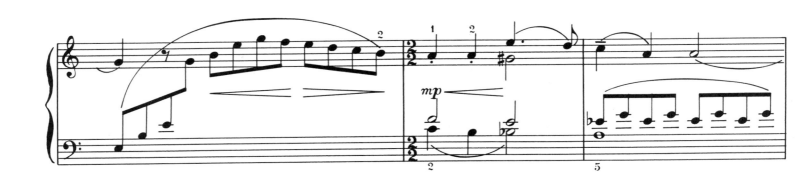

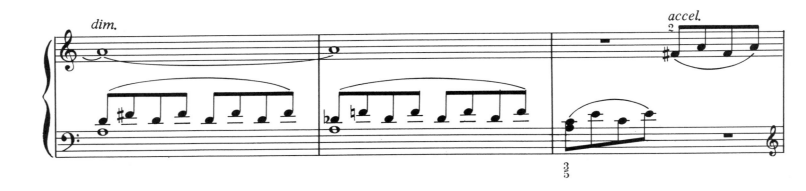

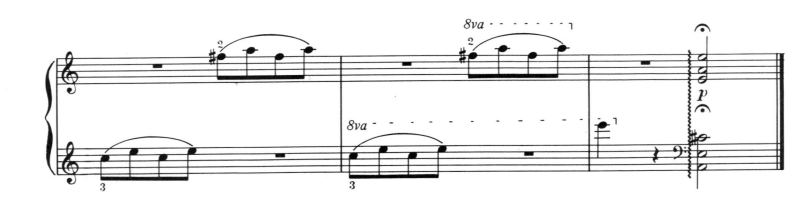

Poco

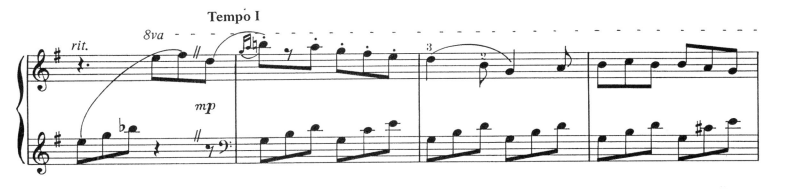

Chromatic Waltz

Music by Denes Agay

Scherzo Sonatina

Music by Denes Agay

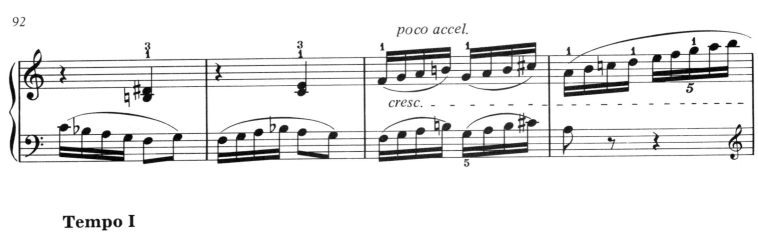

Tempo I

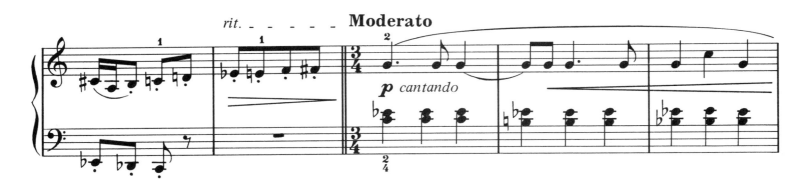

Moderato

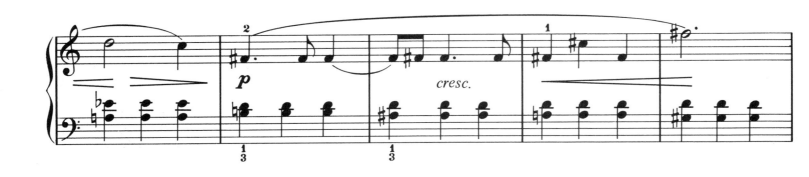

Tempo I

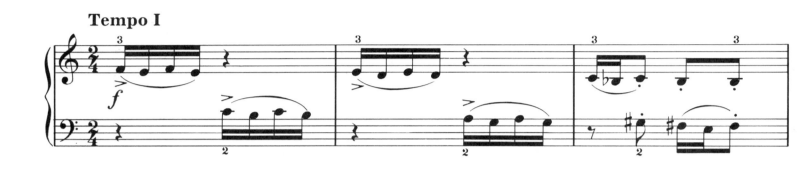

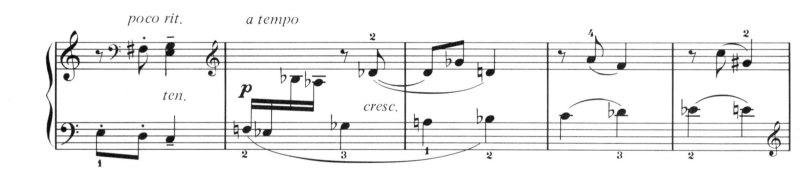

Four Songs Without Words
(Romance at the Mill-Notturno-Torch Song-Canzone-Tarantella)

Music by Denes Agay

Slow, blues-like

a little faster, freely

mf espr.

p

mf

cresc. sempre

rit.

Allegro giocoso

Boogie Variations on "Shortnin' Bread"

(*Duet*)

Music by Denes Agay

SECONDO

PRIMO

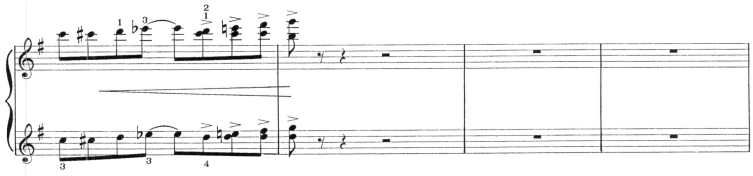

PRIMO

SECONDO

PRIMO

SECONDO

PRIMO

Dance Toccata
By Denes Agay

Secondo

Primo

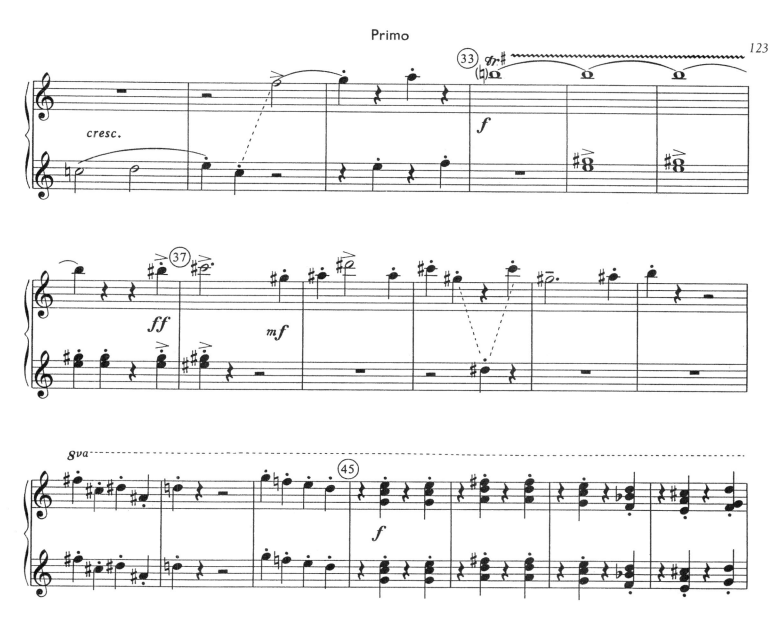

Secondo

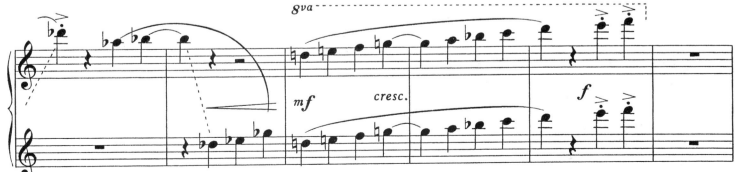

Secondo